"At once personal and philosophical. A must-read for our times, as we flounder with the particular and universal nature of change."

—DEEPA MEHTA, director of *Water, Fire,* and *Earth*

"A profound and thoughtful meditation on who we are and what it means when we change. Vivek Shraya's personal journey touches on the universal and enfolds us all."

—ANNA MARIA TREMONTI, journalist and former host of CBC's *The Current*

PEOPLE CHANGE

PEOPLE
CHANGE

Vivek Shraya

PENGUIN

an imprint of Penguin Canada, a division of Penguin Random House
Canada Limited

Canada · USA · UK · Ireland · Australia · New Zealand · India ·
South Africa · China

First published 2022

www.penguinrandomhouse.ca

LIBRARY AND ARCHIVES CANADA CATALOGUING IN PUBLICATION
Title: People change / Vivek Shraya.
Names: Shraya, Vivek, 1981- author.
Identifiers: Canadiana (print) 20210090693 | Canadiana (ebook)
20210092394 | ISBN 9780735238657 (hardcover) |
    ISBN 9780735238664 (EPUB)
Subjects: LCSH: Change. | LCGFT: Essays.
Classification: LCC PS8637.H73 P46 2021 | DDC C814/.6—dc23

Cover and interior design by Jennifer Griffiths
Back cover photos by Ariane Laezza

Printed in Canada

10 9 8 7 6 5 4 3 2 1

Penguin
Random House
PENGUIN CANADA

To everyone who has given you
the space to grow, to change.

"I am my own experiment.
I am my own work of art."
—MADONNA, 1991

IF MY ADOLESCENT PRAYERS come true, I will die this year. As a devout teenager, I was distressed by my then guru Sai Baba's prophecy that he would die when he was ninety-six years old. I tried to reconcile his eventual death by calculating how old I would be when he said he would die. I would be forty. A world without him was not one I wanted to live in, so my paramount prayer was for us to die at the same time. I prayed and prayed and prayed.

An extreme prayer, but also a rational one. My early experiences of homophobia had already sown the seed of suicide. If I didn't have the fortitude to kill myself at sixteen, or the year after, invoking a future death was my backup plan. One way or another, it wasn't safe for me to stick around. One way or another, I was going to get out.

Sathyanarayana Raju was born in a village in India in 1926. In the months leading up to his birth, strange occurrences were said to have taken place, including the sudden appearance of a ball of blue light that impregnated his mother, and the instruments in his parents' house playing themselves. As a child, Raju was loving and generous to those in need, despite being poor himself. In school, he fluctuated between model student and rebel. He was perceived by those around him as unusual if not extraordinary.

At the age of fourteen, he declared to his friends and family that he was the human incarnation of god. He was henceforth to be referred to as Sathya Sai Baba. "Worship me," he directed. Although some, including his father, doubted this divine revelation, Sathya Sai Baba quickly amassed followers in his village and eventually worldwide.

When my mom was fourteen, Sai Baba was frequently travelling to other cities in India and even visited a neighbourhood home in my mom's native Bangalore. She speaks of how accessible he was then, but how she and her siblings were indifferent to him, writing him off as another orange-clad guru. She regrets this now.

When I was fourteen, Sai Baba was not only our household guru; he was like a fifth family member. Large photos of him were displayed in every room of our house, and visiting friends assumed he was a beloved uncle. I was particularly drawn to the rare black-and-white photos from his youth, fascinated by the evidence that god and I had been the same age once. They revealed a tenderness, a prettiness that wasn't apparent in his contemporary photos. I compared his teenage features, his unruly eyebrows and shy smile, to mine. I was obsessed with knowing his biography, which wasn't unlike a queer coming-of-age: the delightful yet odd child who doesn't quite fit in, the act of "coming out," the disapproving family, the change of name. Was my devotion to him forged in a belief that I too could recast my differences in a new light?

Around the same time, I encountered the word *reinvention* in a newspaper review of Madonna's *Bedtime Stories*. Despite my familiarity with the word *invention*, the appearance of this new prefix confounded me. I pictured the interior of a clock, its cogs rearranging themselves into a new system. Although the reviewer had used the word to describe Madonna's external changes, I instinctively interpreted the process as internal.

From then on, I studied Madonna's career, primarily through vintage copies of her *Rolling Stone* cover issues (my first internet purchases), noting how often the word *reinvention* was used in relation to her. A new Madonna album meant a new sound, a new aesthetic, a new persona, and even new philosophical or religious beliefs.

The new Madonna seemed to transcend the old Madonna, implying that at the core she was a boundless being. This intentional remodelling (however appropriative), this perpetual reconstruction of the self, felt sacred to me.

The most common usage of the word *reinvent* has negative connotations. The phrase "reinvent the wheel" is generally preceded by the warning "don't." This suggests that reinvention is a misuse of time because "the wheel" is already perfect and can't be improved upon. Reinvention is framed as a wasteful and even foolish action, akin to another saying: "If it ain't broke, don't fix it." Is being broken the mother of reinvention?

Living through trauma requires a partial death, or many little deaths. Marginalized bodies continually shed parts of ourselves in order to weather the disasters of oppression.

This is one story I can tell myself: That I was *forced* to change. That I reinvented myself to please or subdue or even mimic my oppressor. I was the proverbial phoenix whose glorified ascension required incineration.

But maybe this story gives fire too much credit. Another story I can tell is that my reinventions predate my trauma and my obsession with Madonna and are rooted in a different mythology. Growing up surrounded by Hindu lore, I was captivated by how gods themselves morphed—from turtle to monkey to eight-armed warrior goddess to Sai Baba—based on the mission at hand. Different desired outcomes, whether defeating a demon or imparting a lesson, demanded different exteriors. As Sai Baba explained, "I have come armed with the fullness of the power of the formless God to correct mankind, raise human consciousness, and put people back on the right path of truth, righteousness, peace, and love to divinity." Reinvention here is once again not superficial, but spiritual. God's outward appearance might change, revealing flashy appendages and weapons, but the motivation is vast and holy.

Even mere humans are born again and again, according to Hinduism, until our cumulative good words, thoughts, and actions outweigh our bad ones. At this point, our individual soul is liberated and merges with the Supreme Soul. Our bodies are mere shells and our soul aches to be free.

This is where homophobia and religion strangely, dangerously overlapped. Both implied that there was something inherently wrong with me, and that reformation could be accessed only through death.

I used to anxiously contemplate the state of my tortured, captive soul at bedtime. Not being able to see or study this vital aspect of my being only heightened my concerns.

There was no way to know just how far along I was, in my present life, on my path to liberation. How many bodies had I disposed of, and in how many bodies did I still have to be imprisoned? What bad acts would set me back, and how far? The process of reincarnation seemed like a game, but without the transparency I was accustomed to from Super Nintendo—no points bar or scorecard. So there was a part of me that didn't want to play at all.

When I was eighteen, I told a friend's dad, who was a clairvoyant, how I prayed to die at forty. He responded, "Then you will never build anything. You will never commit to anything." His gruff warning scared me, but I didn't understand what he meant.

Now I see that he was mostly wrong. I *have* committed—to several long-term friendships, relationships, jobs, and to an art practice that spans almost two decades.

And yet in a way he was also right. Praying to die at forty has resulted in a refusal to commit myself to one static shape. Since I wasn't going to live long, I would live as many lives as I could in the time I had. Reinvention was my way around reincarnation.

Believing I might die at sixteen, or at forty, has meant that I don't take living for granted. I haven't put my dreams or desires on hold for someday. I don't carry a bucket list. "Seizing the moment" has been less about embracing the present and more about understanding that I am not entitled to a future. None of us are.

I no longer agonize or even think about the status of my soul. If I were to have anything resembling a higher purpose, I'd now say that it's to evolve and to model evolution. To demonstrate the beauty of change.

As popular aphorisms about change point out, change is inevitable and constant. Even on a cellular level, the human body replaces itself every seven years or so. But my relationship to change isn't one of fear, resignation, or even victimhood. Instead I consistently *seek out* change, crave it, conjure it, worship it.

A STRONG SENSE OF
STYLE IS ATTRIBUTED
TO CONFIDENCE, TO
KNOWING ONESELF. BUT
STYLE ALSO COMES FROM
INSECURITY, FROM FEELING
LIKE YOU NEED TO PROVE
OR TO SURVIVE SOMETHING.
IF FASHION IS ARMOUR,
STYLE ARGUABLY COMES
FROM FEELING UNSAFE.

A POPULAR TROPE IN mainstream media is the image of a trans woman gazing at herself in a mirror, applying makeup. The message this trope conveys to the audience is that the trans woman's identity is something she puts on, and that she isn't herself—rather, she's really a *he*—before this act of maquillage.

Although I've deliberately steered away from replicating this image in my art, I've always relished the act of transformation. As a teenager, I looked forward to tearing off my house pyjamas and putting on going-to-the-mall attire. The process of changing stoked fantasies for the outing at hand—the conversations to be had, the snacks to be consumed, the movies to be watched. But no party or hangout ever lived up to my hopes, or to my outfit. Because of these disappointments, I soon reframed dressing up as the main event.

Did my love of transformation come from watching, on repeat, the sensual scene in

Batman Returns when Michelle Pfeiffer as Selina Kyle unravels her apartment and stitches herself a slick black catsuit? Or from my affinity for makeover scenes in teen comedies? A case could be made that I identified with the homely protagonist who—by merely whipping off her glasses—reveals herself to be a starlet.

Or maybe it was the way these characters discovered that their true selves had been lying dormant, waiting to be unleashed (unlike the trans girl staring at herself in the mirror, whose transformation is portrayed as concealment).

As much as I love getting dressed up, I also can't wait to return home and slip back into my pyjamas, turning off the social switch and the corresponding pressure to impress. It's the before, the after, and the subsequent that has drawn me to transformation, the opportunity to express multiplicity—that someone can be more than one person, can oscillate between shy secretary and ferocious cat woman, and that no one person is more true, but rather the truth (and thrill) lies in the sum of my parts and in the seeming contradictions among them.

Marianne was my seventh-grade homeroom classmate. She had flourishing rosacea and protruding front teeth, and she wore an oversize blue polo shirt to school every day.

It wasn't just her appearance that made her unpopular. Always the first to throw her hand up in class, Marianne seldom gave the right answer—Lisa Simpson, but without the brains. Not surprisingly, she was regularly picked on, though impressively, she always yelled back at her bullies, which might be why I never intervened. (Or maybe this is the excuse I gave myself—I had problems of my own.)

One day Marianne showed up late for class wearing a black bodysuit tucked into high-waisted jeans. Her dull brown bushy hair was slicked back behind her ears. While the class collectively gaped, our teacher sighed, unfazed. "Marianne, you're late. Have a seat." Marianne swivelled to face us and announced, "Actually, sir, I'm *Suzie*, Marianne's twin sister. Marianne's not feeling well today, so I'm stepping in for her." Her voice had a trace of an unidentifiable European accent. "Sure thing, *Suzie*," one of the boys yelled, breaking the tension. Everyone laughed. Suzie blew a kiss at the class and sat in an empty seat in the middle of the room, not the one Marianne typically occupied.

Our teacher persisted with the lesson, but from where I was sitting, at the back of the class, I could see my classmates turning to study Suzie suspiciously. The boys were especially distracted by Suzie's more sculpted breasts. When they caught themselves staring and realized *who* they were staring at, they scowled and looked away.

As someone who'd recently been inducted into the mystical world of *Days of Our Lives*, I was familiar with the "surprise twin" storyline and was intrigued. But even as Suzie steadfastly remained in character for the rest of the day, and the days to follow, it was clear to everyone that Suzie was, in fact, Marianne.

After a few weeks the blue polo returned, although Suzie attempted to sex it up by tying it on the side above her waist and leaving the three collar buttons open. She appeared to be running out of stamina, exhausted by the relentless teasing: "So how is Marianne feeling these days? When is Marianne coming back?"

On the day Marianne officially "returned" as her unkempt self, she joyfully declared, "Here I am!" Her soon-fallen face suggested that she had mistaken the questions about her health as genuine concern. Instead, everyone was over this storyline.

When I've thought about Marianne in the years since junior high, I've felt guilty for not forming a nerd alliance with her, or for not sticking up for her. (Marianne, if you happen to be reading this, I'm sorry.) As I gained more distance, her performance began to seem less funny and bizarre and more disconcerting, which only compounded my guilt. The way I saw it, Marianne had broken down. Or rather, we'd pushed her to the edge of her ability to tolerate the taunting, to the point that she dissociated from herself and pretended to be someone else, for weeks.

But now, I find myself returning to my initial reaction of awe. Marianne reinvented herself as an act of survival. Even if she didn't remain as Suzie, and no one really believed her, by giving herself a makeover and a new identity she flipped the script. For a few weeks she was under the spotlight, and we were all extras in her teen comedy.

Like Marianne, I too believed in my power to transform—I was convinced that I could change my face. That my appearance was *shaped* by my character. Kind actions would form "kind features," and conversely, cruel actions would cause "cruel features" to develop.

There are many holes in this belief, among them the fact that my nose has refused to shrink in response to any of my random acts of kindness. Another hole is that when I was in junior high, the people around me who were deemed most attractive were often the cruellest. But I'm curious about what made me want to change my face (beyond being a victim of puberty). Was this just another response to my experiences of homophobia and racism, which were teaching me that queer and brown are ugly or "cruel" and that straight and white are beautiful or "kind"? If I could control my appearance, then I could also control how others judged and reacted to me. Or did I imagine I was like a Hindu god who changed their exterior?

Beyond religious influence, I've always believed that the construction of one's image is seldom only about what one does to one's exterior. The making and remaking of my image and style has been about reflecting my interior cosmos.

My fashionista origins can be traced to eighth grade, when I'd spend hours on my bedroom floor after school poring over photo spreads in magazines like *GQ* and *Details*. These were transformation bibles that illustrated how different times and settings demanded different appearances. Eventually, I started scrapbooking my inspirations in lined journals and planning my seasonal look months in advance. My more adventurous ideas needed to be tested out live on the runway (the school hallway), including sporting an onion bag on my head as a hat, weaving a crocheted winter scarf through my belt loops, and wearing unplugged headphones around my neck as a choker (and to add movement when I sashayed).

Through these external experiments, I was developing something internal: my sense of individuality. But also, judging from these particular choices, my personal style emerged in some part from resistance to the mundane. Changing my style was a form of artistic expression. I didn't have the impressive or expensive wardrobe of my white peers, so I learned to create luxury in the mixing, matching, and reimagining. Why should an orange net be doomed to just carrying onions? Why did a scarf have to be limited to being worn around a neck? By elevating ordinary items around me, my fluctuating style did the same for me. Why be one of the boys when I could be one to watch?

At eighteen, I started shopping in the children's section, buying brightly coloured boys' shirts with dinosaurs or Disney characters on them. One day, as my mom and I were sorting the laundry, she asked, "If you don't like being teased, why do you draw so much attention to yourself with your clothing?"

My mom's choice to blame me and my attire for the teasing was consistent with how my exteriority was read and punished at school, except my classmates weren't as direct. Although I didn't have an answer for her then, now I would say that wearing boys' shirts was my way of returning to a time when I was unscrutinized, unscathed. Wearing ultra-tight clothing was my attempt to hug and flaunt a body and its wayward manner and spirit that I'd shunned during puberty. I'd also started coming out to friends as gay but was still struggling with the word and the pressure to make an announcement. I let my fuchsia shirt do the telling.

Despite what anyone did to make me want to disappear, and as much as their efforts sometimes worked, demanding to be seen by wearing clothing that made me impossible to ignore was my way of resisting complete erasure.

As an adult, I revel in changing my style not only as a means to highlight different physical and emotional angles but also to explore personas. I studiously reference my favourite actors and musicians—not as pure mimicry or idolatry. Instead, like a style Frankenstein, I'm eager to observe how transposing someone else's aesthetic onto mine creates someone new.

This is why Halloween makes me uncomfortable: the intention behind dressing up is to scare (or for jest). Why must transformation be monstrous and frightening, or something to be laughed at, instead of an opening for self-discovery?

Queer people learn to hide ourselves at a young age through mastering performance. We know first-hand and through keen observation that the exterior is always a show. Learn from us: You don't have to cloak your fantasies with guises. All clothes are costumes. Come out! Give yourselves more than one day of the year.

When I started teaching full-time, I was anxious about returning to a site of trauma—the classroom—as a Transgender Teacher. But sometimes the only way to change culture is to reinvent yourself. I decided I wanted to be addressed as Miss Shraya, a professional name to formally mark my evolution. It was also a talisman. This new version of my name helped—and still helps—remind me that when I'm in the classroom I'm not teenaged Vivek under homophobic surveillance but Miss Shraya, someone who is fearless, focused, nurturing, and hopeful—a cross between Kalinda from *The Good Wife* and Maria von Trapp, without the singing.

When my feminist friends questioned me about why I chose "Miss" instead of "Ms."

(and thereby setting back the movement), I explained that in the same way I'd been denied girlhood, I'd never had the experience of being called Miss. Deliberately adopting Miss in a position of authority was also an attempt to reclaim a title that's been used to infantilize and demean women.

When I teach, I typically wear dresses on only the first day of class. After that, I settle into my uniform: a white dress shirt with black leggings. In my twenties, when I'd wear the same clothes at work and outside of work, I felt I was never not working. The white dress shirt now marks a clean line between work and play, between Miss Shraya and my non-teaching self.

Historically, the uniform has been a means of both asserting and minimizing power, of both diminishing and highlighting distinction. The uniform is also connected to safety. I'm drawn to the uniform, especially in the class-room, because of these tensions that it embodies

and how they echo the tensions of my job.
I want to be approachable in the classroom,
but as a trans feminine teacher I need to be
cautious about when, where, and how I make
myself available. As a person, I value my individuality, but in my workplace, I'm guarded
about overexpressing my gender. Being at
the front of the classroom, my job inevitably
involves being looked at, but when you are
gender non-conforming, you are also prey to
a particular kind of omnipresent fixation, a
perplexed gaze. So here I choose assimilation
as a means of self-preservation, because the
freedom to express my interiority through my
external choices is a privilege I don't always
have. Wearing the white dress shirt every
single day says, "Nothing flashy going on
here. Just the same old. Now let's focus
on learning."

At the end of this past semester, as I was
wrapping up a portfolio review session with a

student, she asked, "Why do you always wear the same thing when you teach? I was talking about it with another classmate and we're sure you're making a political statement."

Apparently, my strategy to be understated has been unsuccessful. When you're not a man, your appearance is never neutral. Even a white dress shirt is political.

Other questions that women frequently ask me about my presentation include "Did you do your own makeup?" and "Is your hair real?" Are these questions that non trans women ask one another? Admittedly, I adore working with makeup artists, and there's nothing wrong with wearing hair pieces. But the questions imply that deception might be involved in my appearance, and therefore in my self. Or that I can't possibly know how to put myself together, that I must have needed help, because *I'm* not real. I am made up.

The question of feminine authenticity has a monstrously long history. In her book *Hope in a Jar: The Making of America's Beauty Culture*, historian Kathy Peiss documents the association of women's use of cosmetics with putting on a "false face" in the early 1600s, witchcraft in the 1700s, and a legal reason to be arrested or fired in the 1900s for being deceitful, ostentatious, or seductive. And this question goes deeper than mere presentation. Our actions, work, choices, and even character are always under scrutiny, with an assumption of duplicity or fraud.

Why are men not accused of being inauthentic or fake or of going overboard when they grow facial hair or alter their physiques in the gym? If anything, our culture celebrates these changes in men, as exemplified by celebrities whose careers have been drastically elevated simply by getting buff or sporting a beard.

For feminine people, where is the line between being real and being fake, between

being "on board" and going overboard?
Is waxing the hair off your body authentic?
Is spending hours in a salon every few months
to get your roots done on board?

Why aren't we fighting for autonomy instead
of authenticity?

Unfortunately, autonomy is often conflated
with and critiqued as making choices that
seemingly uphold white, sexist, fatphobic, and
ableist beauty standards. So when feminine
people aren't under attack for being fake, we're
charged with perpetuating the standards that
oppress us. Although it's important for each
of us to consider our complicity in relation
to oppressive systems, this is an impossible
binary to be locked into.

Recently I became fascinated by a young TV star
whose transformation has been largely attributed
to lip fillers. I was astounded by what a difference
thicker lips can make to even the plainest of faces.

When I've shared my interest in lip fillers with friends (all of whom are left-leaning), their responses have ranged from a baseline discomfort to annoyance to almost anger. In fairness, women and feminine people are under minute-to-minute pressures to change our physicalities to meet a variety of beauty standards for every part of our bodies all at once, so all of these responses are valid. It's also difficult to know how to support a friend who wants to make a physical change without feeling as though you're supporting the patriarchy, and without being forced to examine your choices and boundaries around your own presentation.

Most of my friends have closed their responses with a statement along the lines of "You're beautiful just the way you are." The way I am, meaning: *Don't change.*

The beauty industry, and its chief enabler, the media, have never been predicated on transparency or autonomy, despite the appearance of providing options. Or rather, women and feminine people have never known full autonomy. Instead, our exposure to misogyny begins at an early age, and involves ceaseless judgment of our appearance, ensuring we're properly beaten down and broken in. Marketing swoops in, also conveniently at an early age, and manipulates us into investing in products, clothing, and treatments that will bestow confidence on us (while implying, as another blow, that the lack thereof is *our* fault). We're encouraged to make choices that will make us look slim and fair, and to do so regularly so that we remain young and current. Then we're mocked for overinvesting in our appearance, for being vain and superficial, though the economy relies on it. And finally, the burden is on *us*, solely, to ensure that our presentations are socially responsible. We are exploited, extracted from, and gaslit at every angle. If the beauty industry were a person, our relationship would be classified as abusive.

Under these conditions, is it possible for us to really ever know what *we* like and value in relation to our appearance? What changes would we make in how we present ourselves outside of capitalist and social pressures?

Boasting about not using a filter (#nofilter) on photos posted on social media is kind of like boasting that you're lazy. If the appearance of the subject of a photo can be enhanced (as defined by said subject), or if the overall quality of a photo can be improved by a boost in saturation, a tighter crop, and yes, adding a vintage or poppy filter, why not use the time and tools to make the modification?

The implication seems to be that the absence of a filter makes the appearance of the subject more "real," and as a result the photo is "better." But *every* photograph is a construction. The subject is always mediated through technology and the gaze and choices of the photographer. This is partly why selfies are unsettling and trivialized. In a selfie, the subject isn't mediated by a "professional" photographer—the subject is, audaciously, the photographer. The gaze and the gazer are one.

The dominant argument against filters or apps that shrink noses and tummies is that some people "go overboard" by making themselves unrecognizable. Such arguments are also made about physical alterations, like lip fillers. Incidentally, all of these criticisms are wielded to invalidate trans bodies.

Similarly, to be popular on social media, users are encouraged to be authentic—use your authentic voice, tell your authentic story. But social media is inherently curated, also a construction. Being endlessly confessional online, for example, isn't really authentic, especially if the goal is to gain followers and likes.

Every portrait of myself (and the responses others have to it) teaches me what expressions, poses, angles, clothing, and lighting I like, giving me invaluable intel about how I want to present myself, both in front of a lens and not. What if we stopped trying to project authenticity and instead admitted that our image and presentations actually reflect an ongoing process of figuring ourselves out? And that this process of learning (and relearning) how we want to see ourselves and how we want to be seen involves stumbling and posturing. Because whether we steer the process or not, our exteriors are always changing, never flat or one-dimensional. Why deny our growing pains and transformations instead of owning them?

REINVENTION IS RELATIONAL, TETHERED TO HOW IT'S RECEIVED BY OTHERS. EVERY TIME I PRESENT A NEW VERSION OF MYSELF, THOSE AROUND ME ARE ALSO CALLED UPON TO CHANGE.

BEST FRIENDS FOREVER. *True love lasts forever.* This is how we're indoctrinated at a young age into a belief that "true" feelings are eternal and unchanging. But longevity can make relationships—friendships in particular—a challenging site for growth. In the absence of protocol or precedent for breaking up a friendship, the implication is that our friendships will and should endure. This is lovely in principle, but when I've changed or considered making a change, I've run the risk of being held back by a friend's expectation that I'm still the same person.

We're generally comforted by the consistency of our friends, not their irregularity or unpredictability. We want to believe that our friends will not only always be there for us and close to us but also understand us, agree with us (most of the time), be recognizable to us.

Years ago, when a new friend and I were planning a trip to Lake Louise, we discussed going horseback riding together. Upon hearing this, our mutual friend, who was also my oldest friend, snickered and said, "There's no way Vivek will get on a horse."

Our mutual friend's assessment was not unfounded. She knew that I'm not an animal person. I'm scared of cats (likely because I *am* a cat), and I prefer to wave at dogs from a distance. But what was exciting about my new friendship and our trip was the promise of discovering that I might be a different person. Perhaps not a born-again animal lover, but someone who might ride a horse, even if only once.

New friends offer the chance to learn about a new ideology, to see the world and yourself through a new lens. To reveal a different side of yourself. My hunger for friendship has been intensified by a desire to know the kaleidoscope of my own possibility.

Of course, relationships aren't merely ciphers for self-discovery, but reinvention typically requires the catalyst of interaction with others. Riding a horse through the mountains was a regal experience that I would never have had without the prompting of my new friend.

Shemeena and I were together romantically for over ten years. If happiness can be measured by how seldom you think of suicide, those were some of the happiest years of my life. We had a rhythm, a flow, enraptured solely in every detail of each other. Sometimes we'd join our hands side by side to marvel at how the orientation of our palm lines mysteriously matched. We weren't politicized and didn't yet use language like "white supremacy" or "misogyny"; we lived a shielded life, laughing our way through working our nine to fives, lunch breaks together, strolls and movies on the weekend. It was everything you see in rom-coms—except starring brown protagonists—and the honeymoon phase was a lifestyle.

In the later years, our profound comfort with each other, the destination that young couples strive toward, started to concern me. I knew exactly what our evenings and Saturdays would look like—where I would work, where she would read, and at what restaurants we would eat. I found myself fantasizing about new relationships. Not entirely because of the person at the centre of the fantasy but because of what *new* represented: the unknown.

I remember telling Shemeena then, *I want to grow*. It was a bizarre, even cruel statement to make when it insinuated the possibility of a breakup. Why would anyone walk away from joy, from the most reciprocal love they had known, for the sake of growth? What did that even mean? Grow into what or whom? And why couldn't we grow together? The phrase "put down some roots" implies that growth requires stability. Solid ground. A foundation.

And yet somehow I believed that I could grow only if I blew everything up.

Looking back now, was the desire for growth an excuse? Was I simply bored? This hypothesis doesn't quite feel right next to my never-ending curiosity about what piques Shemeena's curiosity. There are other surface-level possibilities: I secretly wanted to be with a man. I was secretly a woman. These hypotheses are based on ideas of who I *really* am—that I am really gay and really a trans woman. These assumptions, which may seem to be validated by my current choices and identities, invalidate who I was *then*.

When Adam and I started dating, I wasn't obsessed with him. I didn't sleep with my phone tucked under my pillow, waiting for him to call. I didn't agonize over every word he said, tortured about how he felt about me. I told myself that not behaving in the sometimes unruly ways I had in previous romantic relationships was a sign of progress. This was what it was like to date in your thirties. This was what maturity (and a few years of therapy) felt like.

And yet a part of me felt underwhelmed. I liked him, felt at ease with him, was attracted to him, but I didn't feel stimulated. No spark, no Carrie Bradshaw zsa zsa zsu. This was troubling because I knew that you either have chemistry with someone or you don't.

I was wrong. After a year of dating, a fire was unexpectedly kindled. I found myself thinking about him and wanting to be close to him with more fervour (and thankfully without any angst). Maybe two introverts just needed more time to open up to each other. Maybe I shouldn't have been dating someone only a year after my breakup with Shemeena. Maybe Adam's aloofness was a safeguard in response to sensing my lack of commitment. Either way, I'm grateful that we kept investing in each other instead of calling it quits. Because one of the greatest lessons I've learned from Adam is that chemistry *can* grow.

It's unfair to compare one relationship to another, but now with Adam I see a familiar pattern emerging. Once again, I know what our evenings will look like, what our weekends will feel like. We're as comfortable as a well-worn pair of sweatpants.

Is it time for me to blow us up? In the name of growth? Is the only way to grow by continually creating new relationships? How do we find ways to grow *inside* of existing relationships and older friendships?

Some friendships need to die. Sometimes we're so trapped in old patterns or comforts that we don't offer anything meaningful to each other except history.

When I've broken up with friends or have been broken up with, it's typically gone one of three ways: slowly drifting apart, sudden ghosting, or a fight. Each approach has been heartbreaking.

There's a potential in-between step missing here. In a monogamous romantic relationship, individuals can change their status from couple to co-parents or business partners, or open up their relationship to other lovers. I've found attempting to modify the boundaries of a friendship more difficult. You're either friends or not friends.

One way around this rigidity is to take space from a friend. This is a common tactic in romantic relationships that I've found equally effective in friendships. Creating temporary distance can offer both parties a new perspective from which to assess what the friendship means to you, what you appreciate about it and what you find challenging. When you resume the friendship, you can have an honest discussion about what's working and not working in the dynamic and how to move forward.

The key to reinventing a friendship or to approaching a friend breakup more like a "conscious unfriending" is dismantling the hierarchy of relationships where romantic intimacy is queen. Friendships are integral to our lives, and our friends deserve for us to invest as much—if not more—care or accountability in them as in any romantic partner.

One of the consequences of adapting well is that you can be perceived as indestructible or immune to pain. When Shemeena and I were going through our breakup, one of my friends was bewildered by my emotional flailing. "I always thought you were a rock," she said. A "successful" reinvention is seemingly one that *subsumes* pain, that embodies resilience, one in which the transformation is seamless, hidden. We never have to see inside the cocoon. Maybe we prefer not to.

What might a reinvention that *acknowledges* the pain and history it's born out of look like? In the music industry, the comeback album is the ultimate reinvention. We respect the comeback because it announces that our beloved artist has recovered from their previous mishaps, missteps, and misfires. The language of the comeback doesn't hide the past. Instead, it's eerily synonymous with resuscitation—back from the dead. A comeback album implies that the artist has been born again. Madonna titling her 1998 comeback album *Ray of Light* is both a nod to the shadow of controversy and criticism that landed on her career during her *Sex* book era and a declaration that the eclipse was over.

Can the sentiment of the comeback album be extended to human growth?

Four years before the release of *Ray of Light*, I listened relentlessly to the Smashing Pumpkins' album *Pisces Iscariot*. My ears didn't compute grunge or distorted guitars, so it was surprising to hear the band in a more stripped and acoustic context. One of the standouts for me was "Landslide." Billy Corgan crooning existentially about aging over a finger-picked guitar was a haunting listen.

I had no idea that I was hearing a cover or who Fleetwood Mac was until years later, when the Chicks also covered "Landslide" and I began researching the song's origins. I love the Chicks and their signature twang, but being partial to what I believed was the original by the Pumpkins, I was put off by how overproduced their cover was. I was also fascinated by how different one song could sound when filtered through the voice and musicianship of another, even though the lyrics and melody remained the same. The Chicks' version featured layers of radio-friendly harmonies that, to my ears, diluted

the power of the individual struggle articu-
lated by a single voice.

Cover songs are both wildly popular and
polarizing—because of the familiarity *and* the
differences. At music gigs, I always include a
cover song mid-set, when audience attention
starts to wane. Instinctively, people tune back
in, intrigued by hearing a song they know
delivered in a different context.

After the Chicks' cover came out, I tracked
down the original. Although the Pumpkins'
version remains my favourite, Stevie Nicks's
voice, how worn and wise it sounds, makes the
original undeniably beguiling. Covering a song
is seldom an exercise in fixing or improving
the original. Instead, a good cover shows the
listener a different angle—the beauty of a
melody sung slightly slower or higher, or the
ache of a lyric delivered with less or more
intensity. A good cover reveals to us something
else the song can be or say.

Like the comeback album, cover songs exemplify the balance required in an ideal reinvention. Reinvention shouldn't just discard the old for the sake of the new. Reinvention should honour the foundation of the past and build upon it.

"Landslide" is one of my top five favourite songs, and one of the reasons I'm eternally moved by it is that I hear it as a song about change—at once fearing it, being resigned to the inevitability of it, and also embracing it. Songwriter Stevie Nicks has shared that the song is about the uncertainty of her relationships to her career, her lover and bandmate, and her father.

I remember repeatedly singing this song to myself amidst my breakup with Shemeena through tears and hiccups. We were changing and I was terrified. Terrified that our breakup was reckless, terrified of losing her in my life, terrified of the other side of the mountain.

But "Landslide" calmed me down.

I cherished every day of dating and being married to Shemeena. We were committed to not recreating our parents' marriages and dynamics, and we painstakingly carried this commitment into our divorce. We believed that a breakup didn't have to be messy and cruel, that the care we had always shown each other could still be centred. Together we went apartment hunting, helped each other move into separate places, packed and assembled our individual furniture. We even had a divorce party with our close friends where we celebrated what we'd learned and loved about our marriage.

Our breakup has unexpectedly allowed me to fall in love with her again and again. It was agonizing at first, but I've loved witnessing her build new intimacies and hearing her process her feelings from a different position. I've loved spending time in her apartment and learning about her individual design and aesthetic choices. I've loved sharing our goals every New Year's Day and being able to call each other out in ways that only two people who intimately know each other can. I've loved preserving some of our traditions (seeing a Christmas Day matinee), letting some of them die (going to a kitschy chain restaurant on Christmas Eve), and creating new ones (spending Christmas together with Adam).

One of the secrets to growing with someone is changing the language and ideas about relationships and endings. Shemeena and I *have* in fact grown together, but our growth is limited by the word *breakup*—its implication of permanent fissure—as well as the understanding of it as only a culmination. Even the word *ex* is inaccurate in our current configuration. Beyond its relegation of a relationship to the past—often a negative past—*ex* carries the added sonic and visual components: saying the word invokes an image of something, *someone*, being crossed out. But we're very much in each other's present, definitive check marks. And although I have several close friendships, *friend* also seems to fall short as a description, because it erases our history.

When we were trying to find a more appropriate word to describe our current relationship, we discussed how much we'd grown to love the word *partner* in our marriage. It implied being partners in crime, us against a white, biphobic world. What was the word for a relationship that spans between past, present, and future, partner, ex, and friend? When I suggested we fuse *friend* and *partner*, we both snorted. *Fartner*. Silly as it was, it was exactly what we needed to move through the pain of transitioning from one kind of relationship into this new, unknown one.

I like to think of relationships as plants that have potential for regrowth and renewal. Maybe my relationship with Shemeena needed to be pruned to improve our overall health and allow us both to keep growing. Maybe our roots actually needed more space and we just needed to be transplanted. Every year we celebrate the day we "broke up" (our "fartnerversary"), because it's not the day our love shrivelled up, but the day our love propagated.

Adam and I have been dating for several years, and each year I feel a little more enamoured than the one before. But with all long-term relationships, it can be easy for the fucking to morph into cuddling, and over time your lover unconsciously becomes the roommate you occasionally spoon. One of the ways we've side-stepped this de-evolution is by reinventing who we are in bed. Although the roles we play aren't particularly transgressive or inventive, flipping from being a manager or a postman or a grocery stock person allows us to see each other and to desire each other in new and tantalizing ways. It also allows us to live out desires that weren't accessible when we were both growing up, that are still not possible. I have zero interest in being a coach in real life, but I like imagining and embodying the strength and confidence of this role. Some reinventions are best relegated to and fulfilled as fantasy.

When I'm at my most pessimistic, when I'm in conflict with myself or a family member or a friend over a longstanding issue or pattern (like my concerns about being too demanding, or not prioritized), I wonder if change—true interior and complete change—is actually possible. In these moments, I remind myself to think about my dad.

Many years ago, when my brother, Shamik, turned eighteen, he began asserting a newfound autonomy in ways that led to regular fights with my mom about his schoolwork, his curfew, and his friends. Fed up, he decided to move out. This was a blow to my mom, who interpreted the move as a failure on her part—failure as a mother to steer him in a direction that was aligned with her values, especially getting a post-secondary education. I listened as their fights amplified in the days leading up to his move, until one day I snuck down to the basement and quietly called my dad in Grande Prairie, desperately hoping I could implore him to intervene.

"Shamik is moving out this weekend."

"Yes, Mom told me." He sounded just as surprised as I was that I'd called him.

"Are you going to come home?" I respected my dad as a parent and occasional authority figure in my life, but we weren't close, partly because he often worked out of town.

"I can't come home. I'm working."

"Your son is moving out and not in the best circumstances. Don't you think you should be here?"

"You know I can't come home. I'm working," he repeated.

In the months that followed, when my mom and I sat together for dinner and I watched her cry over her food in a state of mourning, my feeling that my dad didn't care for us cemented. I mentally wrote him off.

Once I entered the workforce full-time in my mid-twenties, I developed a new appreciation for my parents, or rather an empathy for what it might have been like to work while being a parent. I first directed this compassion toward my mom, who'd done the bulk of the parenting, by recasting all the times I'd classified her actions as "nagging" instead as expressions of legitimate frustration. In time, I began to see that my dad had also played an essential role in my life, even if it wasn't the role I had wanted him to play: he helped provide our family economic stability, which was the role that had been modelled to him by his father.

After I moved to Toronto, he started sending me sporadic emails, always in caps lock, saying, "SO SORRY I WASN'T THERE FOR YOU WHEN YOU WERE GROWING UP." My responses ranged from suspicion to resentment. It's hard to process a shouted apology, let alone one that arrives so late.

And yet, when he turned sixty, I decided to surprise him by flying home for his birthday to honour this milestone with him. He was genuinely moved and grateful.

Since then, he's started taking more of an interest in my life, asking questions about my work and my art. When I called home in my twenties, if he picked up, he would say, "Hi, here's your mom," and pass the phone to her. Now when he picks up, we chat a bit about the weather and the news. When I'm at home for a visit, he always wants to know how many copies of my books have sold. He also tries to engage me in a conversation about sports, which I oblige by asking about the few hockey players I remember from the Edmonton Oilers' glory days: "How is Esa Tikkanen? Where is Jeff Beukeboom these days?"

My dad has reinvented himself as a parent in his sixties. I never imagined that this kind of change was possible. His transformation contradicts the popular idea that aging equals being set in your ways. He's proof that change can happen at any age.

Without taking away from the work my dad has done on his own, and without fully knowing what motivated him to change, I believe that my empathy was one catalyst. My ability to see my dad as more than the sum of his mistakes, and my willingness to celebrate his life regardless of how disappointed I was in him, may have allowed him to see himself as a parent, and to engage with me, differently. Reinvention requires this kind of empathy from those around us—to be seen for more than our shortcomings.

My dad recently started apologizing again for not being present in my teenage life. "You don't have to apologize anymore. You can let go of your guilt," I told him. "You're present now. That's what matters."

It's equally important to consider what factors make change socially legible. Who is allowed to change and whose changes are seen or valorized? If you're a man, any change you make, regardless of the timing or significance, is perceived and received as a radical act—because nothing is more miraculous than the bending of the supposedly immutable. This explains the popularity of the scene in movies and TV shows when the conservative, homophobic father is dramatically redeemed by his eventual acceptance of his queer child (unlike the mother figure, who is never offered the same glory for her steady support). How often do we fail to recognize change in women and femmes because we're expected to be adaptable?

Before Shemeena and I got married, I struggled with the implications of forever. When the only certainty is change, how do you promise eternity to someone with any certainty? In my case, when I couldn't see a future for myself, how could I ethically promise to share my future with someone else? Moreover, my primary model for commitment was my parents, who I was convinced had overpromised. When I confessed my concerns to a friend over a late-night coffee, she responded wisely, "You can't promise forever, but you can promise to be honest." I have since clung to this advice and tried to extend it beyond my relationships, because it subtly acknowlededges that truth changes.

THERE'S SOMETHING
UNTRUSTWORTHY ABOUT
SOMEONE WHO IS
CONSTANTLY CHANGING. A
THIN LINE BETWEEN DEVIATE
AND DEVIANT—BETWEEN THE
ACT OF VEERING AWAY
FROM EXPECTATIONS AND
BEING NEGATIVELY DEFINED
AS A PERSON BY
THIS VEERING.

ALTHOUGH I ACTIVELY PURSUE opportunities to reinvent myself, I'm also wary of the glorification of reinvention and adjacent terms like *rejuvenate, revive,* and *renew*—all words you can find in a brochure for a holistic spa retreat. Reinvention is aspirational, and the idea that you can enhance your overall quality of life through it has been commodified. Madonna has even monetized her reputation for reinventing by launching both a tour and a beauty cream with the word *reinvention* in their names.

Given the root word of *invention* and the implication of repetition invoked by the addition of the prefix, reinvention is inherently tied to productivity: bigger, better, or improved. These hierarchical or capitalist inclinations are troublesome and unappealing to me. I don't want my next shape to be necessarily better; I want it to be different. I want to change for the *experience*—and for what I can learn from it—rather than for any quantifiable "results."

One of the most difficult aspects of witnessing the more recent stages of Madonna's career and public life (including her racist comments, further appropriation, and general cultural cluelessness) has been the ways that, from the outside, she seems to have stopped reinventing herself. In 2019 she released her fourteenth album, called *Madame X*, a persona that appears to be an amalgam of everything she's already shown us. Given that her last number-one single in the U.S. was in 2000, is there a connection between her falling popularity and her failure to reveal something new?

I've been growing out my hair and dyeing it blond for half a decade. As someone who used to proudly change my hairstyle once or twice a year, I worry about what this "commitment" says about me. Have I lost my edge, grown complacent? Is settling into one hair-style emblematic of settling in general? I used to wonder if Madonna would ever run out of new hairstyles, and now it seems that both of us have. But do I have to make an outer change to prove that I still have an inner fire?

There are changes I can instigate, and then there are changes instigated by factors outside my control. Given that baldness runs in my family and is a part of aging, I'm constantly fretting about losing my hair. I try to remind myself that stress is one of the causes of hair loss, so I pretend not to get anxious when I notice the cluster of strands in my hairbrush or splayed in the nooks and corners of my apartment.

My inevitable hair loss will trigger an unwanted change in my presentation. For years, I've been pre-emptively researching wigs, weaves, pieces, vitamins, and drugs.

I give myself an Ayurvedic head massage every week, drink aloe vera water shots with cumin, scoop a teaspoon of diatomaceous soil into my daily smoothie. I don't know whether any of these steps are helpful or working, but I'm desperate. Despite believing that there are many ways to be feminine and that gender is a social construct, I worry: Can I be bald and still look femme, still be desirable, still have a healthy career?

Of all the changes Madonna has made, her aging has been the most unwelcome. Over the past twenty years, I've heard many snarky comments about how she should just retire. Go away. Be invisible. Like aging women in general. In her own words: "I think the most controversial thing that I've done is to stick around."

Sometimes I worry that I've secretly clutched my prayer to die at forty because of my own internalized ageism. Because if I don't die, once again I will be expected to disappear.

When Lady Gaga emerged in the 2000s, I was offended by the likening to Madonna. It was unfair to both parties to compare an emerging artist to an icon—or to compare two female artists at all. Mostly I was disturbed by Lady Gaga's frantic changes from single to single, video to video. I felt like I was watching a salon on acid or a wardrobe having diarrhea. The speed of her transformations suggested a lack of commitment to interior change. The intentionality of reinvention that I revered seemed to be mocked, debased. This wasn't reinvention. This was desperation.

In fairness to Gaga, the ongoing disposability of women and female artists, combined with the increased saturation (and therefore disposability) of pop music in the internet age (almost two decades after Madonna launched her career), has meant that reinvention has become more common and expected, particularly for female pop artists, as a means of staying relevant. Being irrelevant is synonymous with aging. If you can't be forever young, you have to find a way to be forever new.

Reinventing myself in my art practice allows me to be continually inspired and growing, and to dodge boredom, because the process always involves the challenge of learning a new skill. My artistic reinventions are also, in part, a way of addressing the responsibility I feel to audiences who steadily support my work. I strive to offer you something a little different in every project as an expression of gratitude, and to hold your interest in case your attention span is as slim as mine.

As I age, one of my sharpest fears about my career, aside from the loss of ideas, is that I will peak, haunted by the saying "You're only as good as your last success." In capitalism, the conflation of self-worth and success is deliberate—you're of value only as long as you're producing. And additionally, for feminine people, only as long as you're changing.

When a project of mine is a success, I worry that it will be my last, that henceforth my career will flatline. This concern is reinforced by the ghost of my twenties, when the interest in my work was nominal. I don't want to return to that time. How much is my desire to change and to experiment in my art practice actually a subconscious response to sexism and, now, ageism?

But despite the pressure to change, it's not entirely clear to me that audiences are interested in reinvention over familiarity. Or rather, how much change is *too much* change? After all, my commitment to constant reinvention has arguably been one of my biggest impediments to building an audience and acquiring institutional support for my art career. I'm regularly told "You do too many things" and asked "What are you doing *now*?" or "Can you repeat your last project?" What I hear in these statements is "Why can't you do just one thing?" or "You are too much." These messages are best exemplified by the most common compliment I receive: "You're so prolific." A quantitative observation instead of a qualitative one, akin to saying "There are so many colours in the sky" instead of "What a glorious sunrise."

When you consider the world's most popular artists, they habitually do one thing over and over again (and consequently, they do it very well). Madonna is synonymous with reinvention precisely because of how anomalous it has been in the broader music industry, and her frequent changes are often regarded with suspicion or skepticism. Some argue that she uses reinvention to distract from her lack of talent, to be provocative and grab attention.

Meanwhile, no one expects Dolly Parton to release an electronic album, or Danielle Steel to write a political thriller—and if they did, I suspect their fans would be disappointed. This is an oversimplification, as these artists also work in many other fields. But there's a unified core to the work these artists produce that allows audiences to hook in, get comfortable, and become loyal. Successful expansion or diversification can be attained only when a strong, clear, and consistent brand is established. Rihanna moved into makeup and lingerie only after she established herself as a global pop star.

In my art career, I strive to *de*familiarize, bouncing between forms, navigating and releasing multiple projects in multiple genres simultaneously. Even though there are thematic threads that run through my body of work, one of my main objectives is to generate new ways to approach them. As a result, I've been told that my output is confusing and hard to keep up with, which is code for difficult to connect with. I've also been warned about oversaturating the market. What feels exciting to me—shifting from genre to genre and medium to medium, and creating as often as inspiration strikes—can feel destabilizing to others, like a lack of space or time for someone to sink into the work and its ideas.

Because of my creative approach, I've been described as wearing "many masks" or "many hats." Both the mask and the hat suggest that my modes of expression are mere accessories, decorative elements that I impose upon myself, or in the case of the masks, that I use to hide myself (and also to deceive others).

In the *Mahabharata,* Lord Krishna momentarily bestows divine vision upon Prince Arjuna so that he may see Krishna's supreme form,

Vishwaroopa, a massive cosmic being with innumerable heads and arms. This act reveals that it's Krishna's *human* identity that has been cloaking his multi-faceted divinity. It also exemplifies how the inability to see and accept multiplicity is often tied to a limited vision. And even with enhanced sight, multiplicity must be conceptualized through thousands of additional appendages for it to register.

My mom worked in the same position at the same workplace for over twenty years, while my dad was a chronic job-hopper. My mom positioned the stability of her job as ideal and my dad's shifting employment history as hazardous. What if it were the other way around? I don't want to over-romanticize the employment hardships of a brown immigrant in the 1980s, but I now find myself drawn to my dad's path (even if it's tied to male privilege). What if he was, in part, more adventurous or more aware of what he didn't want, more driven to seek out what he did want?

Our culture values stability, security, consistency, longevity, discipline. The opposite makes us feel confused, unsafe, helpless. A long marriage (however unhappy) is considered a success, whereas divorce is still seen as a failure and final. We also glorify the proverbial long walk on the beach as the ideal romantic pastime, a lengthy education history as the ideal employment qualification, the lifelong friendship, the dedicated novelist or filmmaker, or even just living a long life. Dying young is considered a tragedy without any real examination of *how* the life was lived. The longer the time invested or even passed, the greater the worth.

What do we get from endurance over exploration? Is it legitimacy, the ability to assert authenticity? Why is it that exploring is so often synonymous with frivolity, dabbling, indecisiveness, being noncommittal or unstable, or having a mid-life crisis, and endurance isn't synonymous with complacency or stagnation?

Time and rigour are luxuries. Not all of us live with the same clock.

SOMETIMES GROWTH
IS ACHIEVED BY BEING
SOMEONE ELSE—SOMEONE
YOU'RE NOT, EVEN SOMEONE
WHO, AT FIRST GLANCE,
YOU DON'T WANT TO BE.

AS A KID, HAVING a plethora of gods was thrilling. Unlike other boys, who collected hockey cards to learn about their favourite players, I mentally gathered data about each god—their different names, functions, powers, aesthetics, animal vehicles, and legends. But in Sunday school, I was eventually corrected. Hindus actually believe in only *one* formless god. Different exteriors provide humans with different entry points, different options to elicit attraction and devotion. If you weren't into the blue bro with the bow and arrow, maybe you could connect with the ethereal swan-riding, veena-playing goddess.

This is how I explain the appeal of being a multidisciplinary artist. It creates multiple opportunities for connection. If you have an aversion to poetry, may I move you with music or provoke you with photography?

But unlike Hindus, I don't believe in a single, stable, true self. One of the reasons why the popular advice to "be yourself" can be confounding or intimidating is that we're vast and immeasurable. When you consider all the people you've been this year, this past decade, this life, can you easily pinpoint which self was most true? Most authentic?

Two of my family's favourite movies are *Sister Act* and *Mrs. Doubtfire*. Together we've watched them countless times, and doing so has also become a christening ritual for when we add chosen family members. In both films, the protagonists pretend to be people they are not. Despite the hilarious tests they face in maintaining the pretense, their new roles end up being a catalyst for real growth. Whoopi Goldberg's character becomes less superficial and selfish, and Robin Williams's character becomes a more responsible and considerate co-parent.

When I returned to university at thirty-four to complete my masters, I felt as though I was posturing as a grad student—old, unintelligent, and out of place among my classmates, who proudly quoted Butler and Foucault behind their open laptops, talking in circles while many of my professors were silent bystanders. In addition to the imbalanced atmosphere, I was overwhelmed by the piles of dense assigned readings that professors seldom foregrounded and that didn't seem to take into consideration our capacity. Concerns about workload were dismissed by my professors with a "welcome to grad school" shrug. Many of my classmates openly shared that they were taking anxiety medication between classes, or were on anti-depressants, or some combination of both. I occasionally saw students leave class in tears and heard others crying in the bathroom. In one of my classes, a student disclosed that she had a fear of public speaking, so our professor asked her to do her presentation with the lights off and directed us to look down and avoid eye contact with the student, instead of finding a more workable (and less humiliating) accommodation. It seemed as though being stressed and sleepless was an acceptable and even necessary component of higher education. I was resolutely opposed to this "pedagogy" and considered dropping out every day.

But as the weeks passed, the life smarts I'd developed by working full-time and managing deadlines for over a decade kicked in to compensate for my lack of book smarts. I focused my attention less on being frustrated by my reading lists or my professors' demands or "the system" and more on what I actually needed to do to complete the program, namely what I was going to be evaluated on. This was not the experience I was hoping graduate school would be, but by faking it as a grad student, I acquired valuable information: I learned what I would want my classroom, my teaching practice, and my students' experiences to be like if I ever became a professor.

The problem with understanding the self as singular is that the only way a new self can be legitimized is by disavowing one's past self. I'm true *now* because I realize that that past person was false. This feels akin to the way I've heard friends say, after a breakup, "I don't think I ever really loved him." What if it was that their definition of love had changed, or that they themselves had changed and were unable to continue being the person they were in their relationship? What if in that previous relationship, in that moment, it *was* love? A past love doesn't render a future love less true. Multiple loves can be true. Multiple truths can coexist.

Similarly, most coming out narratives imply or declare that the self prior to coming out was confused and unhappy because they were not being true to themselves. Like when newly gay friends state they weren't actually attracted to their previous opposite-sex lover or partner. This might be a genuine assertion, but even in queer communities there's pressure to deny bisexual attraction, or rather, bisexuality is commonly read as still being in the closet. I don't want to dismiss anyone's experience, but how often do we embrace the narrative of a true self because it's expected of us? No one advises you to "be yourselves." There's only ever one self to be.

An argument could be made that reinvention is an act of running away from oneself. But again, this presumes that we have a singular true self, and that any change is a detour or diversion from that self. Instead, reinvention is an ordinary human process, and you need only to begin cataloguing the many different people you've been to realize how constant and pervasive it is. We tend to chart our selves through stages of human development—childhood to adulthood—or the decades of our lives. But there are many other ways to document the versions of ourselves: through the hairstyles we've had, the fashion choices we've made, the music we've loved, the cities and houses and neighbourhoods we've lived in, the friendships and crushes and partnerships we've nurtured, the schools we've attended, the jobs we've had, the art we've created, the beliefs we've held.

When I examine the people I've been, none of them strike me as less or more true. Of course, there have been times when I've restrained myself, or even knowingly not acted in alignment with my values, but I'm not willing to concede that there was something false about any of my past selves. Deeming parts of our lives as false or true has consequences. Living a life of self-judgment, compounded by other judgments of good and

bad, right and wrong, ignores nuance and traps
us in an unforgiving prison. And too often we
judge ourselves retroactively instead of taking
the time to develop a clear picture of why we
might have acted the way we did.

I would rather argue that I was as honest as
I could be within the boundaries of whichever
environment I occupied. I will never know what
choices I would have made in a different environment or in the absence of external pressures.
It feels more important to honour the resilience
of my past selves than to dispute their integrity.
If there is a lie here, it's the lie of a solitary
authenticity. I'm not more true now, but my
circumstances have changed: the acquisition
of new language and coping skills, and stable,
progressive employment, allow me to be a
different person than, say, when I was unin-
formed, not seeing a therapist, or working a
front-line job. I'm not more true now, but my

values have changed: I'm more aware of injustice, of the spaces that restrain me, of the necessity of saying no.

I'm not saying that we shouldn't monitor and evaluate our actions. But reflecting on our past selves can't be just an exercise in longing for or condemning who we were. Instead, it's an invitation to appreciate everything and everyone that got us to who we are now. It's also an opportunity to identify and limit how often we tell ourselves one-sided stories about the choices we make. We need to be more empathetic toward ourselves, to give ourselves the benefit of the doubt instead of chastising ourselves for being untrue. We need more room to make mistakes, more room to try, more room to fail. Living "authentically" often doesn't allow us to live curiously and compassionately.

And reflecting on our past selves also allows us to dream who we want to be next.

—

When I was considering changing pronouns, what appealed to me most about the word "transgender" was the implication that an individual had *transcended* their assigned gender. In my case, this transcendence suggested an infinite resistance to masculinity.

Five years after coming out as trans, I worry that I conflated transition and reinvention. Despite my efforts to complicate my own beliefs about femininity and womanhood, and to explicitly express this complexity in my presentation and art, public transness has merely transplanted me from one box to another. Admittedly, because I wanted to be believed, I sometimes perpetuated the idea that I was now, at long last, my true self. The promise of possibility that I believed was latent in a transgender identity was stripped by the popular understanding and pressures around transition. Now I feel stuck having to forever embody and assert a standardized "trans womanhood."

This is a dangerous admission because of the widely held assumptions that trans people are confused, uncertain, and change our minds.

But I'm not confused. I am certain—that I want to keep changing.

I often wonder how I might have approached my transition differently five years ago. At the time, I announced on social media that I was now using "she" and "her" pronouns. I didn't announce a new identity label because I hadn't selected one. None of the options felt entirely right, and I didn't think it essential to formally reclassify myself. I didn't even change my name. But others immediately began referring to me as a trans woman. I felt unsure about correcting everyone each time this happened, because a part of me wondered if the label would fit in time. I also felt that the assumption of "woman" was my fault for choosing "feminine" pronouns. And I worried that my discomfort with the label suggested the possibility of my internalized transmisogyny.

Perhaps I might have explicitly chosen to identify as "non-binary" had it been a more prevalent term then. But it now seems foolish that I thought I could safely express my femininity without adopting a formal identity.

Identity labels can be invaluable as a means to self-actualize and connect with community. They're also crucial in naming inequalities. But if the question is "What comes first: self-identification or oppression?," my experience has been the latter. Othering often begins with labelling. My labels are often acquired as a response to being labelled, given to myself never out of real choice but always as an act of reclaiming.

The more labels I've "embraced," the more apparent it is how little they benefit me, how

much they serve the dominant culture. White-
ness, for instance, doesn't need to be named at
all; it's ubiquitous and doesn't require "understanding"—it just is. When I'm speaking in
some spaces, I might refer to myself as gay
instead of queer because I know how provocative "queer" can sound, and in using it I run the
risk of detracting from my message. Similarly,
sometimes I'll say I'm bisexual instead of queer
because I'm purposely trying to promote bi
visibility. And sometimes I've called myself a
trans woman because I know that this will be
clearer than saying trans feminine person of
colour or even just trans. All of these choices
I make for the comprehension and comfort
of others.

But which one am I? Gay? Queer? Bisexual?
Trans woman? Trans femme? Non-binary?
I am whichever one makes sense for the
particular moment and social context I'm

situated in. I am all of these identities and none of them.

The marginalized individual is systematically concretized into an identity—through either discrimination or the guise of acceptance— as a restraint, because there's nothing more frightening than fluidity. At some point when the individual "chooses" an identity in defiance (even rejecting identities is a kind of identity), we're then gaslit through arguments for the need to eradicate labels because "we're all human." But by this time we're fully attached to our box.

Oppression followed by the violence of identification jointly act as an antidote to reinvention.

There's another self I want to address: the ideal self. The person you imagine you would be if you had more time and resources.

Meet my ideal self: she has a regular meditation and yoga practice, reads every day, and flosses every night. A seemingly simple list, and yet this version of myself has remained elusive for over a decade—until this past year. Largely owing to the flexibility of my teaching schedule, I've managed to successfully incorporate yoga, meditation, reading, and flossing into my life. At long last, I have become my ideal self. Hooray!

And yet I don't feel any happier. My life doesn't feel more meaningful. In fact, I feel much more fulfilled when I slack off from crossing out tasks on my idealized to-do list to see a friend or a movie. It turns out there's more to life than living your so-called best one.

Our ideal self is actually holding us back, not propelling us forward. Like our true self, the notion of the ideal self once again limits us to one ultimate self, instead of giving us room to grow and explore alongside our evolving circumstances and desires. It limits our future. Once we've arrived at destination Ideal Self, there isn't anywhere else to go. To some, this might be an achievement. To me, it's stifling. I hope that I'm *not* actually my ideal self now, because I want to know who else I can be, what other layers I might shed or add.

What if, instead of trying so hard to find our true selves or to become our ideal selves, we thought of each self as valid in its own right, a necessary stepping point to the next one?

What if we were to alleviate the pressure of aspiring to be our ideal selves (or using the unattainability of our ideal selves as a way to berate ourselves) and instead focus on creating ideal experiences each day?

I want to imagine a world in which we can change, shift, and play as often as we choose, and where this multiplicity is honoured instead of cause for suspicion. I want to wake up in the morning and ask myself not "What do I have to do today?" but rather "Who do I want to *be* today?"

WHEN I REFLECT ON a life of many forms, desire is the pulsing force that links them. The desire for love, respect, connection, touch, and growth. One of Sai Baba's teachings is that disciples should keep "a ceiling on desires." I remember first hearing this message at a spiritual retreat and being flooded with a wave of desires—a Slinky, a new tape deck, a stack of pancakes from my favourite diner. Many other religious schools like Buddhism and Christianity also propose either keeping one's desires at bay or eliminating them altogether.

But what is a life without desire, without wanting? The moments when I've felt an absence of desire haven't felt like contentment. Instead, the absence of desire has felt more like the absence of self. Living demands wanting. The obsessive pursuit of one's desires can be harmful, but there's nothing wrong with desire itself.

Morphing from a musician to a writer has been my most significant pivot as an artist so far.

I often credit this reinvention to the death of my dream, the heartbreak of realizing that my music career would not reach the heights I'd aspired to. But it was also driven by a creative spirit that was still alive, still wanting to be expressed.

Reinvention requires both a kind of death and a desire to keep living. And so at its core, reinvention is inextricably linked to hope: the hope that we can find another way, take another shape.

Sai Baba is no longer alive. He died at the age of eighty-five, not at ninety-six as he prophesied. Although I'd long ago distanced myself from him and his teachings and community, a part of me still grieves. I think I believed that Sai Baba and I would have some kind of communion. That one day, he would acknowledge all the love I beamed in his direction and declare his love for me. That I wasn't just one of thousands in a crowd, that he *saw* me. Maybe he would even invite me as a special guest to sing for him in his auditorium. This will never happen now. He died early, without me, and I'm still here, caught in the implications of my old prayer.

I wonder when the death I prayed for as a teenager might happen. (On my fortieth birthday? One of the days leading up to it?) I'm also afraid of the implications of *not* dying, of making it to forty-one: god didn't hear my prayers, god doesn't love me, and I have no great spiritual pull or power—the final blows to my religious child self.

Does a prayer I made to someone who is now dead still count, still hold? If so, can a prayer— a wish I made repeatedly and reverently—be undone? What will it mean to lose the exit strategy I've clung to for most of my life? What might it be like to live without suicide on call?

After all, the secret to my not taking life for granted has been living with desperation—*living desperately*. Would I lose my drive, settle into the apathy of believing tomorrow will come?

Or is it possible to reinvent a future worth living, not a life for the sake of impending death, but a life for *life*'s sake?

If so, please let this book be a new prayer. One to rewrite the old ones, one for more growth, for more change.

For more life.

ACKNOWLEDGMENTS

Thank you, David Ross, for being a believer and tireless champion.

Thank you, Brendan Healy, for our conversations about reinvention.

Thank you, Rachel Letofsky, Nicole Winstanley, Trisha Yeo, Adam Holman, Erin Wunker, Morgan Vanek, Derritt Mason, Shaun Oakey, Jennifer Griffiths, Ariane Laezza, Lilly Wachowski, Elliot Page, Deepa Mehta, Tanya Tagaq, Anna Maria Tremonti, and my forever muse, Shemeena Shraya.

I am also grateful for support from the Alberta Foundation for the Arts, the Canada Council for the Arts, and the Thelma Margaret Horte Memorial Fellowship.